W9-BTD-600

DATE DUE

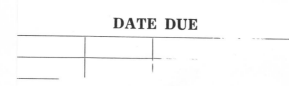

# MORE UNDER SATURN

THE WESLEYAN POETRY PROGRAM: VOLUME 58

# More
# Under
# Saturn

By

WILLIAM DICKEY

**WESLEYAN UNIVERSITY PRESS**

*Middletown, Connecticut*

Acknowledgement is gratefully made to the following periodicals, in the pages of which some of the poems in this volume were first published: *Abraxas, The Atlantic Monthly, The Carleton Miscellany, Epoch, The Hudson Review, The Iowa Review, The Minnesota Review, MSS, The New Yorker, Poetry, Sallyport, Saturday Review,* and *The Southern Review;* and to Twowindows Press and The Windhover Press, the original publishers of two of these poems.

The poems "The Anniversary" and "More Under Saturn" were first published in *The New Yorker.*

The poems "At the Middle of It," "The Bullhorn," "Parliamentary Procedure," "Rehabilitation: The Lion" (under the title "Rehabilitation"), and "Sonnet: The Platonic Form" were first published in *Poetry.*

The poem "Suburban" was first published in *The Southern Review.*

Hardbound: ISBN 0-8195-2058-6
Paperback: ISBN 0-8195-1058-0
Library of Congress catalog card number: 70-153102
Manufactured in the United States of America
*First edition*

This book, again, for Shirley

# CONTENTS

# PART ONE: ADVICE

Give your name awkwardly, the first name first.
Punch the interrogator.
Eat the notes.

If a man answers, hang up.

If a dog answers,
                    Kiss him.

[He will be someone you know
bringing news of me under
a
hopeful
disguise.]

## HOPE

At the foot of the stairs
my black dog sits;
in his body,
out of his wits.

On the other side
of the shut front door
there's a female dog
he's nervous for.

She's the whole size
of his mind – immense.
Hope ruling him
past sense.

## BEING PATIENT THE WRONG WAY: AN ACCOUNTANT'S STORY

1.
I guess my whole problem has been that I can't compete.

2.
When there was only the one moon in your sky I was very happy.

3.
It is like me to be careful in recording this exact goodbye.

In people, nothing is clear. They knot together
and a steam comes up from them and hides them.

Their lettering is tribal, hard to read
unless you allow them the ownership of your closest blood.

More and more each year the refracted moonlight
slivers among them: which shadows are its sure shadows?

Goodbye children. If we meet from now on it will be
in the light of the crystal lattice of an equation.

History begins where I leave you. The historical moon
is a mountain of stone piled upon stone piled upon stone.

They move with deference, each being aware
his body is himself first: to be even partly the other's,
even to give comfort to the other, must be moved with care

so there can be no recklessness in their undressing:
no haste of entrance into a blare of light
that cries: here is perfection mirroring perfection!

In a night that has withered, and under quieter stars
that have aged along with them, they must some way constrain
what each knows to be the other's entirely mortal fear.

Therefore no fury of ownership
or the child-voice crying "Forever!" They are lent
for the time until their expressions close in sleep.

And they conduct themselves with a hesitant ceremony
of gentleness, touching and speaking to one another
through a dark they do not know whether to call love or pity

but that shakes their hearts, so when most they would be
hands and lips they could not tell from one another
loss kisses them, and they touch through harm and care.

You cannot be anything or anywhere forever.
You and it change: the death-music for Queen Mary
slips down the Thames; silt, in the estuary
starts closing the ports inland. Nothing, however
central to your fact or imagination, supremely clever
or self-evidently secure, but the unintentional airy
snowfall of time drifts down on it and its ands bury
whoever you were most sure of: whenever, whatever.

Only as you can abandon to the idea then
your many-sensing body, the sanctifications you allowed
mind and blood-color of being, only when
sweet tastes in the mouth fade, all of the self's sweet mouths
      fade,
will the mute time you were your part of be said aloud,
its voice made out of the self you have made unmade.

Who teaches love
how to be cut
when the flower tries
to leap from its root?

Grandfathers, strong
only in their descent
weigh on it. Time
is their whole argument.

Even of those, not one
himself to blame.
The death of his fathers always
dying again in him.

Love hopes for you,
but the deaths interrupt.
Safe under every garden
its graves are kept.

1.
The sickle of the moon.

2.
Old doubts, returning.

3.
My wife's soft breath, asleep.

1.
Fretful and sick, you ask
"Do they remember me
at my old house?"

Illness makes believable
all desertions; I
might die, love someone else.

If the world failed that way
it would help to think
you could go back

ignoring all those years
that tried to tell us we
lived in the same place.

2.
Yes, they remember you.
Would have to, even though
the photographs are burned

of your hair done the old way
of your dark husband in
his young uniform.

Having loved you they
cannot will themselves
to entire indifference

but turn in the night sometimes
when your light step
touches their dreams.

3.
"Do they remember me?
Would they believe me if
in my thin summer dress

I should go back to them
saying the years between
held no authority?

saying I knew myself
even from childhood, still
uninterrupted, still the same

and that I needed them
in that remembered world
still to stay the same?"

4.
No, the night has gone
where you left them; marks blur
of the fire

on the riverbank.
Rain and the winter's ice
wash them away.

And the figures have stood, turned,
begun to walk down the streets
of new towns

where you cannot be heard
now, with your far voice,
calling their names

5.
Fretful and sick, you long
for reassurance, want
everyone to forgive

what is not unforgivable,
only no longer there
to be forgiven. Caught

in their own time
faces have changed,
lips spoken assurances

to a new night
in which the agreements of the body
have been re-made.

6.
Nevertheless, sleep.
And as your eyes close
in hurt uneasiness,

as your face grows
hot, like a child's
under the weight of the dream

I tell you again that
even when their voices sound
unreachably far away

they still remember you,
your laughter, how you were
at your old house.

After you are asleep, and the night's quiet
smooths out the room I listen to your breath
making clear to me that I am alone.

Day says the opposite: how I am part
of institutions, of shared important rooms
full of companionship and dialogue,

of the identical words of a language shared
by everyone I meet. Then *I* am shared
like a small sun, and warm fluently.

And home to evening, the world of
two people's talk, unintelligible outside
the circle of candlelight and the drawn shades.

How each of us, talking, makes the other real
by knowing what word will follow, accidentally
speaking with the other's turn of phrase

until bedtime comes. You yawn, look up
for my kiss, huddle the blanket close.
You shut your eyes, and I turn out the light

and walk into a house altogether empty
except for myself, the same solitary
figure walking for years from room to room

asking a baptism from the wide dark,
a star to have meaning, an explanation
to link me entirely to your sleeping breath.

But the necessity to remain myself
is the only answer on the tongue of midnight,
said unemotionally through the lucid bells.

I love you when you are sleeping, even though
nightly we must ask each other's leave to wander
through different dreams. In the cold house, alone

for another hour, I listen to you breathe
outside me, a separate fact, until I too
am permitted sleep, the comfortable disengagement

of knowledge and awareness, and can be dead till day
lets us out of ourselves, till the congratulating sun
marries our names and our languages around us.

It was your smell that, for a day after, I carried with me.
My body smelled not of me but of you. The train
ticked over its crossings, stopped. In all its noises
I heard, suddenly and bewilderingly, your voice.

That was six years ago, the damp riverbank,
the Midwest storms massed, raining like an indictment,
the attacks of telephones, old interruptions talking.
Out of that, at your voice, I came to this different world.

Now, with the formal furniture, the black puppy quietly
lying at the door, the flames of the candles steady,
we are held by our reflections in the rose-colored wine —
a civilization of agreements, a closed place.

Thousands of miles away, the summer storms
still race in their green light. The night trains hurry on
across Canada, their noise empty of voices.
The old telephones busy themselves with the old words.

Here, in the Pacific evening, the puppy stands up
suddenly in the doorway and barks toward the dark street,
protecting what has come to include him. Six years, now.
I cannot tell his voice from the room's voice.

I cannot tell your voice from my own voice.

# PART TWO: OBEDIENCE SCHOOL

He takes his own pulse. It is a thing he
often does, and why not? His
pulse is central to him.

If that little swelling
ever gave up the ghost, who
would buy meat for the angry nest of babies?

Who would keep his proud
superior wife, the one with the grimaces,
stalled somehow short of actually shedding blood?

Having the car parked, he
takes his pulse, hands over the keys to
the young attendant, who

guns the car up the ramp
faster than a married man
is allowed to drive.

Impossible, when
the grass sings
to remember
blood like teeth,
the sharp
forearm's weight.

Impossible, when
the moon is a good
nightlight, the sun
has aprons on,
the stars spell
"Nice. Nice."

Impossible, when
the sky pats
my leaves, puts
green in my cheeks,
not to kiss it back
and flower.

This is the mind's Ellis Island; ideas
with swart faces appear, speaking no English.
We enjoy watching their pain and confusion
at being categorically misunderstood.

They have come off the cattleboats: ideas
with bombs for eyes, stuttering according to
old patterns of hope. Facing them, smiling,
we are like rolled umbrellas that have taken root

or like many married swivel chairs. Ideas,
innocent inside their noisy garlic sausage,
egg each other on to the naturalizing kiss,
which fails. Powerful as memory, we stand

all outside-in and backside-out. Ideas
learn to live faintly in a country of no air,
or sail home muttering over the electric water
to die insane in their aboriginal huts.

How over Oxford
at  midnight
the clocks disarrange
the hour, sound
out their differences,
agree to disagree.

What's time to
these pondering
stones, to
the clear towers
suggesting truths
to the night air?

Away in North
Oxford, this
city's lesser end,
I light a match,
look at my watch,
sleep.

What's truth
without time?
Exact towers rise
minute by
right minute
in *my* country.

When the idea of form
emerged, Adam,
nipples gilded with pollen,
short mouth open
for the obedient fruit, said:
"Now there is distinction between quick and dead."

Eve, helpmeet, knitting
hammocks the trees
badly needed, breasts
going "Purl!" with her industry,
thought once, said:
"Superfluous. Send it away."

When the idea of space
as a great envelope, well
licked by God, came
to Adam, he
flattened his belly muscles, said:
"Rightly understood, then, time is a thing."

Eve, fellow parishioner
of the glade, groped
for her petit-point,
irrigated fruit trees,
set sunshades, said:
"This yellow antagonist must be tamed."

When the idea of category
came to Adam, he
distinguished arms from legs,
then left from right, saw
polarity function, said:
"Let us rejoice in the law of names."

Eve, bothered
by tsetse flies, by
great herds of antelope
in the kitchen, said:
"Into the stewpot, beasts!
Wipe that identity off your face!"

Adam, cracking
pecans with his biceps
demonstrating how
the gluteus maximus works,
timing his lymph nodes, said:
"A watch implies, strongly, a watchmaker."

Eve, shelling
peas in a leaf, cutting
green beans into one-inch lengths,
culling wormy turnips, said:
"We have more than enough to do
without deflating the clouds."

*Ultimo*, when the idea
of guilt came to Adam, he,
shocked at himself, covered
reproachable parts with leaves,
came to his opposite, said:
"The long agony is defined."

Eve, plucking chickens, gutting
fish, putting snake meat in little jars,
rattled her tasting spoon, said:
"Get me an apple, there's
something this dish needs, I
hate insipidity."

Probably even
the day completed
was better than
the day hoped for
would have been
if it were completed.

And since even
the day completed
*is* completed
and so surer
than what has to be hoped for
that must be enough.

It is a flat rock, only a flat rock.
It is not the head of a flat snake striking out.
It is what it is, not a thing it intends to be.

Nobody but you, given
in every situation to expect the worst
ever looked at it and thought it began to bite.

Already the world is difficult enough:
bears lecture on forest fires, simple domestic cats
predict you will be the next Lord Mayor of London.

Once it spreads past the animals everything has to go:
the maidenhair fern saying "Stop or you'll get me pregnant,"
or your mother "Why can't you get married to some nice stone?"

It is only (repeat for emphasis) a flat rock.
It is neither the head of the worm Ouroboros,
nor, in the opposite hysteria, not there at all.

It is what it is and what you aren't; be thankful
there are things you don't have to be; keep saying
(always with thanks): "A rock. Just a flat rock."

I wake to the same room in the same world, watching
a snake swallow a snake. Too big for its normal mouth.
It unhinges its jaws to get the victim in.

I was dreaming of a bower-bird that arranged
a garden of love-trophies, the embellished skulls
of its enemies, laid down for it to dance on.

Or I was dreaming of *maîtres-d'hôtel*
curved till the tips of their tail-coats met their mouths,
displayed in a poisonous, elaborate jelly.

I dreamed of what, to the exactly civilized man
makes life worth while: of *Robert's Rules of Order*,
white and negro toilets, agreement of subject and verb.

I wake  to find only this snake swallowing this snake.
How will the bower-bird know whose skulls to choose?
Am I only an enemy of my enemies?

1.
There are the men who make important statements.
They are blond men running to well-distributed fat.
Their voices are marbled like the most expensive beefsteaks.

Underneath them, chewing at their ankles, sending
rockets to fire up their monumental gilded legs
are the edgy men, the blind mice who eat up statements.

2.
There are the women with impervious fronts
that loom like warheads, the women who send their breasts
like double loaves to go plump on the conference table.

Underneath them, the thin flat women with beaks of tin
read grey books, nervously flicking through the pages.
They smile at the recipes for boiling flesh.

3.
I do not say a moral inheres. I only
say there are men who bassoon forth cumulus clouds
and women like punctures who peck at the first whole note.

And women like dirigibles, fat, self-advertising
who keep in marsupial pouches little men
to whom they devote, when they think of it, a tear.

4.
Well, how to resolve this? Citizen, alas,
I am too busy at being a syndicalist king
to hope to instruct, or even to entertain you.

So I suggest you meet my accomplished wife,
the nun in the black net stockings. She is wise,
and whatever truth is, she should manage to explain you.

# FOR EVERY LAST BATCH WHEN THE NEXT ONE COMES ALONG

Next door they've finally brought home the new baby.
Well, my wife says, carrying him over carefully
for a tour of inspection, would you look at that for two weeks!

It's true he's a good baby, big, fine head of hair.
Look, says my wife, his navel's healed up already
and his you-know-what's bigger than the two-year-old's.

I don't hear much from this baby late at night.
He's too big to be fretful; fill him up with milk
and he just hums comfortably on through till morning

while his two-year-old brother cries, deliberately
wets, goes babyish, tries to crawl into bed with
mother and daddy, get back into their flesh,

all of which is anathema to the pediatrician
who knows how the two-year-old statistically
can't be allowed to slide. Up, two-year-old!

Let's get you back on your feet while there's still time.
The world's no raisin bun aimed straight at you.
There's always a new contender for the playpen.

Though I still feel sympathy for you. Who ever wanted
that excessive baby? Who wanted him to arrive
with that vulgar head of hair? Who wanted him to be

carried around the neighborhood, the mothers saying:
Big babies are good babies; would you look at that perfect navel!
Would you ever believe the size of his you-know-what!

What ought to be admired, then? Not the children, surely,
who are undisciplined energies, smashing their tricycles
into each other, screaming like machinery screaming.

And not the mothers, spreadeagled on the porch steps
discussing Crisco and the social status of policemen,
the huge rollers of their hair bobbing above their chat.

Nor the two together, for the mothers alternately
like pop-up toasters cry warnings, "Don't do that!"
and then relapse, while the children do and do.

Off somewhere in night's perimeter, the fathers
fidget with their flies. Can they call themselves at once
fiercely masculine and yet easily understanding?

No one can tell, no one having seen them since
the last surgery of begetting. They have paid in their time
at the bowling alley, have guiltily given blood.

Around stand, range on range, the mixed frontiers
of the architecture, a wilderness crossed by nomads
on thin caravan routes that lead to the real cities,

and the genius of the place, the aborigine
is the woman in the next apartment who hates her son
and says everything twice. "I'll stew him." Pause. "I'll
    stew him."

What ought to be admired? The vague sea fog
obscuring the precision of the planted palms?
The wind, harrowing up the brief grass clippings?

I'll go live
on the moons of Mars
busy around their planet
not far out
high speed

taking with me
for all assistance
only a copy of selections
from Addison and Steele

A man
if that's what I am
and not an invention
needs in his life
some abstraction
nowadays

Deimos and Phobos
never touching
but each with an idea
of the other's
relative position.

Spectating.
At all times
enjoying their bright watch.

1.
Something knocked at our mouths, asking
"Is this where my home is: my home the idea?"
That was action asking: the whiner at the  mind's door.

2.
Let us behave like a ton of lead or a ton of feathers falling
from the Tower of Pisa. Let us act like transparent shoots
    spreading
in the root cellar, unintelligent but armed.

3.
We cast actions into the mirror of indifference
that distorts by accident only: dwarf or giant
swim in that cup of silver like the same drop.

4.
Comfort yourselves. Nothing that we have done
was exact or final, not even our acting selves
that escape now into the soft not ever decided past.

cats & dogs
     come     witness
          I haven't hurt you

I am a lover of animals
I am well known to be a lover of animals

and I have never hit
     any one of you

          except teaching, teaching

**THE INSTRUCTOR HAS NOT FOLLOWED THE LESSON PLAN VERY CAREFULLY**

The motor grinds & won't catch.
Nowhere worth going to: so the car thinks.

And I think. Once there was punctuation
worth listening to. I was used to that & I said:

Here are all the commas you will use up in a normal life.
The students bit at my wrists & ankles &

a wild deer burst into the office & bled to death
kicking the files to mush.

PART THREE: APOLOGIA

**1.**

It is to require the balance of the mind
as the hawk meditates between wing & air
their outward & inward motions intensely stilled

No further resolving, further irrelevance
of the chalk parallels evading across the blackboard
or the fish that will die rather than breathe plain air.

Rather: it is the tightrope-walker, steep
exhilaration of self in the enemy medium,
that permits the air *its* experience of joy

Rather: it is the air's otherness that demands
self a dimension — to be *neither* the cloudy god
nor the ignorant lake of tears in which he drowns.

**2.**

I am not to indulge myself in the animals'
briefer creation, the public fits
of the decorated bull-boys, those soft wicks
who set fire to themselves with their manual applause:
as if the game of the horn were a final cause.

Back through gold branches they die down to myth.
Their final animal takes them by their mouths
with its sea of sperm & in that mess they die:
vessels who would not stand to their steely choice
& must shrink under the weight of a whole voice.

Slashing with blood the sea gorges & mounts.
Its flat eyes try to enumerate the shore
& its blankest animal voice beaches & moans
"I am yours, Noman, who sought me, salt, grave:
neither man nor woman: an instant of the blind wave."

**3.**

If train A goes 50 mph to the NW
there to be intersected by a line tangent to circle B
what is the result, expressed in breasts, apples & bleeding
    ulcers?

In the perfectly square room with the iron nipples
there is only the electroencephalograph whispering:
"It is by system the pretty ladies are brought low."

East & West, from the towering statistical poles
of what we call for convenience IBM Male & Female
there is a data flow of some interest

for those who choose to be interested in such things.

## 4. CANOPUS, VEGA, RIGEL, ALDEBARAN

Those are the names of stars. Protected here
in our quiet room, in the intention of our sleep
immediately and most surely locked together
by the simple current of our circling breath
we lie secure, yet naked to their distance.

If they spoke, the echo would tumble endlessly.
If they came down, ponderous voyagers
from the utmost edge, we would be many times dead,
our bones resolved past idea to vibration,
before in our air the weight of their first step stood.

Like winter animals, curled for warmth and comfort
close to each other, we have become a system
circling a point that sleeps in the air between us
and upon which, sphere beyond sphere, willingly centers
the formal dance of a Ptolemaic night.

Otherwise there might be nothing, only the unnamed
undomesticated stars as a slow crawl of light
scribbling across nothing, ourselves only as the dead
accident of a darkness without occasions,
in which, growing old and separate, we lie.

**5.**

"I can't get interested
in the way they keep
talking about morals
in all those poems."

An old complaint of readers
who walk the seashore
discovering now squids and
then sometimes their own limp pricks

and unable for long years
to tell one from the other.

**6.**

There, in the bloody heavens, a crazed star
with the face of William Blake, portends, portends.
It says in its carbon voice, "Enjoy yourselves."
What, after our lessons in the antinomies?

The voices of the deranged comets that delight in
excitements of plague time, a voice out of the Coal Sack singing
"All flesh is the education of the grazing mouth."
This chorus has been by some so dignified

that the earth is turned to a generation of mirrors,
small and intense, each reflecting William Blake
who lolls in an armchair, stroking his artillery,
while the red cats of intuition lap his feet.

In the high salons the candles have been snuffed
by swift footmen of shadow; green against absolute darkness
God and a tiger cry out, each one unable
to hear the other, to be other than alone.

**7.**

I call upon the shade of Pope
& on the shade of Swift, to keep
the dimension of the house intact.

I call on Reynolds, for beginning
his lectures, "Gentlemen," for seeing
reason among the serious stars.

I call on Johnson, for refusing
that flattering world of accident
that by our merest absence dies.

On Pope for the knowledge of a place
for man that is neither here nor there
but posed in the hesitance between.

On Swift for the will, unsatisfied,
watching the night, no matter what
the seductions of the storms of sleep.

**8.**

*Nihil* ex *nihilo,* from nothing nothing.

To be only the body thus making the body nothing
hard veins on the backs of the hands     crisp eyebrow     nothing.

The nothing that jerks in the assaulter's inturned mind.

It is Miss Click at the switchboard, her hands busy
with the male & female plugs, assisting in conversations
in a language she does not believe she can understand.

**9.**

So that if, at morning, I am in the midst
of my wife's warm body, the collection of that gesture
does not end ideas about the roots of being.

Neither when, at noon, controlled by the rational sun,
latitudes center themselves precisely in a right sky,
are the commentaries of the flesh forbidden to cast shadow.

Not even at dead night when the pack ice weights &
thickens to its most opposite poles shall we be allowed
wholly the blind luxuries of our categories.

**10.**

Delicately & with all misery they lie down,
their pale eyes large but unseeing, their thin faces
parallel on the pillow, but in no way intertwined.

Each has explored the universe of his private body,
the uselessness of the nipples, the secret hair.
Each is as contained in himself as a man can be.

Outside, at a distance, a noise like a music box
plays *Frère Jacques*. Then the voices of children
excited, crying over and over, "Ice Cream Man."

In the room the vision of themselves stares straight ahead,
intersected by nothing but a sound of the other breathing,
which, if one wishes, one can suppose unreal.

**11.**

Night of the brute creation: it all sleeps.
Night of the infolded wing & the spent song.
In the trees, that are the mothers of permanence
that strange blood dreams, gathering to its end.

High, in the Victorian watch-tower
over the city, the unexhausted mind
submits itself to the requirements of its forms
so that the night may continue & be secure.

The mute field mice, somehow expecting winter,
seek out granaries; over the night sky
an occasional searchlight flashes. Back & forth
we move into the decisions of our times.

**12.**

So full of sleep are those who lose the way
that they wander, under the bent eaves of the night
into the shadow only of a spectral moonlight
that seems to them more enduring than the day.

So full of darkness that the natural sun
is to their eyes an injury, a fierce stone.
They cannot keep themselves safely their own
under the inquiries of that broad noon

and so will seek the entry underground,
the unmoved shore, the silent and unmoved water,
where the echo of speech is thinned, the echo of laughter
turns to a thread of vacancy, no sound.

Until even the memory of the shape of day
is less than shadow to them, and their breath
dreams through their nostrils the transparent death
that, full of sleep, now leads them on their way.

**13.**

Then it is the stalwart footman I admire
who holds foursquare to the corners of the evening
his candelabrum, triumphantly ablaze,

the city gathering its pieces, the dark woman
throwing over her shoulders a cape of silver shadow,
she and it excited by the electric night.

In the galleries of the old ruins, something live
starts remembering itself, puts out its hands
that move like intelligence in the shafts of darkness.

In the pitfall of the least alley a face smiles,
acknowledging darkness as its own opponent,
against which it will be beautiful, like the moon.

**14.**

Always the old wild one, my mother, in names of sable
circles the Greek hills, meat dripping from her mouth.

Always, across the alley of what is real,
there is the slight tremor of her husband saying
"Lunchbag, lunchbag," to the interested night.

**15.**

Upon each other's presence the opposites
build themselves: the stepped ziggurat
rears into the steep zone of responsive heaven.

High over his audience, the equilibrist
balances on one finger, and so awakes
the air into a finger that replies.

Opposite upon opposite, it is the dance
in which one partner can never become the other
nor become less than a mover of that pattern

which is the mind, dancing with the flesh it marries,
wisdom dancing with the occasions that require it,
the rising moon, dancing with the dark night sky.

# PART FOUR: MORE UNDER SATURN

My masters & doctors, you begin resignation now.
You stand, in full summer, praised by a formal crowd
that has used you & understood & misunderstood you.
Everyone wipes his face with his handkerchief. The
President asks the students' grandparents to stand up
& be honored for what they have paid for. You too are honored,
as we sweat like calm people in this very benign air.

As if at a stilled Bethesda. The pool, the inane pool,
that could heal everything if its surface were to stir.
The young lame look at the old lame with incomprehension
like ducks ready for imprinting. Have I spent years following you
as my father-&-mother, & you but a constructed thing?
Has each agreed not to be friendly, & to live nowhere real?
When I believe that I know it is less than what you taught me.

I remember Forster describing the human chess game at Cracow;
the figures larger than life, but meaning less than it
towed from the board by little human mechanisms. Night.
Is there a God-center in all that blackness?
The shadow figures rise to their shadow honors,
reminding us where we are: this is an open network:
no mouth can be assured to open & pulse blood.

Lloyd Reynolds & John McGalliard & Don Macrae,
my masters & doctors — you few representing so many —
as I robe myself in the alleys of the Cow Palace
to pay a mediaeval deference to an occasion
conducted in no language actual to the mouths of man
I ask still for your validation. There is a ceremonial
death we may eat, bitterly but I hope together.

After all these years, what have I understood?
Only that I love you: a love imperfect & angry
whose only accessible god is the Christ of the Locked Way.
You will never be my completion: never, never!
Yet summer gathers us in the shadow of its blue day.
No one has given me more than what you gave me:
sometimes the belief to continue to begin.

You are a man falling forward,
running as hard as he can to keep his body under
the absurd point of his fall.

All around you the trees are nothing:
epiphenomena, because they are passed so quickly.

What would happen if you stopped, and stood for years
at the edges of the Ice Forest, in the barest growing,
listening to what is frozen at the center of your true seed?

Much lost; nothing so far replacing.
Falling can tell you that you are very much not someplace.
It hasn't told you that you are not someone, yet.

1.
On the street-corner
across from Macy's
identical platinum blonde
twin midgets.

2.
In the parking lot at Akron
three gay boys
all deaf-mutes
camping with quick hands.

I read the newspapers.
I'm not a fool.

What if I do sell matches?

I could be selling other things
like you, or some fat Chinese dogs to eat,
or myself to you, or even myself to myself.

I could be selling statues
of General Dwight David Eisenhower
in life-size life-colored plastic.

I read the newspapers.
I'm not a fool.

What bothers me is how
little by little those statues
start to sound better
than all the other news.

## THE GIRL IN THE DIRTY MOVIE

has red fur
a bed, dress
eventually the most
elaborate lace garters
more eventually, not that

then only
on her right foot
as she moves to music
arbitrary to how she moves
an Ace bandage

the men watching
out of their darkness
cut that foot off
quickly

red
fur
red
fur

Rituals are greater than what they talk about.

Now we are speaking only to the amendment.

There are fires in the Indian wilderness outside
& they are capable of letting us shred
each other's flesh & lick the blood from our pronged fingers.

The main motion has been withdrawn &
the substitute motion has now become the main motion.

In a mask reaching from my feet to above my head
sewn with the dried penises of men I have killed in battle
I encourage you to war: I piss strongly into your hands of blood.

Christening is a perception of system: not what is said
but a shape expecting the idea of what might be said.
It is time. I own myself wholly only in long time.

Skulls urgent on the dirt floor
are asked to suckle at their victorious women's breasts:
skull-milk, skull-milk: there is a thick semen.

The Chairman recalls the attention of the House.
There is a question to be put formally to the House.
The question is whether to terminate debate.

is his real mouth. The boy
has become what he was only talking into
& what he was only saying.

He said it. Now there is probably no
saving him from the advances of the arch police.
Who loses himself is theirs
who professionally lose themselves.

Now not even his sweat, the saltwater breaking
at his armpits & groin,
not his blood, breaking,
makes him real.

The police run forward. Their excitement quickens,
sweat rimming their nostrils
& the galvanic foam glistens
along their sea-borne manes.

The boy throws himself into his mouth for
the last time he can do it. It
uses him. Nothing more uses him. Now

he too is his whole machine under the blue day.

## A HOUSE: FOR SHIRLEY

I see it's no real use to ask for attention.

A poem is a house in the mind. I live there.
Archimedes lives there. I don't ask
you to admire him.


But if you *should* admire him
then the house has walls hung with tapestries that show scenes of great
    love, of great effort & accomplishment
and on the floors there are silk-knotted carpets intricate with patterns
    of thin noble men in profile carrying hawks, & with patterns of
    evasive but promising moon-breasted women &
in the sweet warmth of the jasmine garden outside there is the song of a
    nightingale who pierces his endless breast with his endless beak for
    love and pain.

That is not Archimedes, you say, looking at me with misgiving.

No, but it is the idea of a house, and all houses are houses.
We *live* there.

Again, no use to ask after attention.

But look.

Here I am, drawing this simplest, only this simplest figure in this
    plain white sand.

Come inside.

Comice pears poached in red wine with spices.
*Suprêmes de volaille à brun.*

Crusoe saves what is possible.
Wine & food: a composition.

Outside the hide yurts & the babies
dead of kwashiorkor, of parental battering.

Madame, we will go down the river at 9 o'clock
under a studied midsummer sky: all blue, all blue,

& the music will be with us & we will live
only in the music, saying:

thus we feed something even to those who rot & drown.

Of course it sounds cold.
It is cold.
Every year spent on the ground draws that much more of the
      first warmth from our bodies.

What did you think would insulate you against time?

    *

I walk out into the winter garden.
It is the root vegetables —
beets, potatoes —
the russet apples wrapped separately in newspapers and packed
      in old barrels
on which we live.

    *

        Dead cabbage-stalks
that grew up fast out of the fleshy, leafy fruit
stand like a field of dry clubs.

Who's there, to hit at?

    *

The sky appears to be indifferent. If it spoke,
"Love me," it would say. "You keep alive from now on
only on how much of me you can refuse to hate."

## FIRST NIGHT GONE

The dog should be here.
Someone should be here.
Not just the little hiss of the lamp
and the furnace whispering.

Too much whisky and memory
in an empty house.

Where you are, I hope you are better
and rest, and that your fear eases a little.
It's good to be quiet sometimes, to fall into quiet
as through and beyond slow water.

And outside, where you are, the dog will race
through country sunshine, inquisitive and free.

But I hope you can pack your bag and come back Wednesday
and I not frighten you or fall from you
into absence of person, of affection or belief,
into a no-self, missing your face and voice.

"What do you need me for," you asked, "really?"
I need you to come home, because you are home.

Where would I go?
What would my hands and feet do?
The hands gloves, the feet only old shoes.

The dog walks up & down the street carrying a sign "Divorce."

Then we would have a garage sale
& sell the dog
& sell the memories of your Uncle Fred.

& sell the red lacquer chest from Kyoto
& the bed.

Nothing is love that is a mess of agreed-on things.

I take your wax hand & I put it in a bureau drawer,
& I put the taste of your mouth into the Aqua-Jet
& on my knees wipe the hair out of the bathtub.

And I put back the seat belts in the front seat of the VW
        that you never put back
& I walk the dog that you never walk any morning
& the dog every morning shits in front of the three-year-old
who says "Mommie, what is that dog doing?"
"Mommie?"

Even the adding machine won't do the taxes.

Why should I know how you fix an adding machine?

Moving, at the far edge of my window,
a moon the shape of an old face
fades and brightens
as the fog drifts in front of it.

Not a skull,
only a face starting to imagine
what its skull might be.

It is the only thing in the heaven.

It is not helped or accompanied by any stars.